ADHD PARENTING: A COMPREHENSIVE GUIDE TO RAISING HAPPY AND CONFIDENT KIDS

DR DHEERAJ MEHROTRA

Made with ♥ on the Notion Press Platform
www.notionpress.com

Contents

Preface

Parenting a child with ADHD presents unique challenges, but it also offers growth opportunities, both for the child and the parent. **ADHD Parenting: A Comprehensive Guide to Raising Happy and Confident Kids** *is designed to be an essential resource for parents seeking to better understand and manage ADHD in their children. This book emphasizes 200 practical, easy-to-implement tips aimed at helping parents foster positive behaviours, establish supportive routines, and strengthen their relationships with their children.*

The guide delves into the critical aspects of ADHD, focusing on the importance of structure, patience, and understanding. From managing impulsive behaviour to improving focus, the strategies outlined in this book are meant to support parents in creating a balanced, nurturing environment where their child can thrive. It addresses behavioural challenges and the emotional needs of both the child and the parents.

*Whether you're just beginning your journey or looking to refine your approach, **ADHD Parenting** provides guidance and encouragement. We aim to help parents feel confident and empowered as they guide their children toward success, fostering happiness, self-esteem, and resilience. Together, we can navigate the ADHD journey with understanding, compassion, and optimism.*

www.authordheerajmehrotra.com

ONE
INTRODUCTION TO ADHD PARENTING

"The hardest thing about ADHD is that it's 'invisible' to outsiders. People just assume that we are not being good parents and that our child is a brat, when they don't have an idea how exhausted we truly are." —S.C.

An Introduction to ADHD Parenting

Parenting a child with ADHD brings unique challenges and opportunities. This introduction focuses on three critical topics: understanding ADHD, the emotional journey of parenting an ADHD kid, and the value of early intervention.

Understanding ADHD.

ADHD is a neurodevelopmental condition characterised by persistent inattention, hyperactivity, and impulsivity that impairs functioning and development. Parents must understand that ADHD is not the product of poor parenting or a lack of discipline but rather a complicated disorder influenced by biology and environment.

Children with ADHD may struggle to concentrate on tasks, follow directions, plan activities, and manage their impulses. They may appear agitated, speak excessively, or have difficulties waiting their turn. These behaviours substantially impact their academic performance, social relationships, and daily activities.

Understanding the nature of ADHD allows parents to handle their children's behaviours with understanding and patience. It also allows them to effectively advocate for their child's needs in school and social contexts. Recognising that ADHD appears differently in each child is critical for designing tailored methods to assist their strengths and challenges.

"The way I handle my child's behavior may look permissive to you, but constantly scolding does nothing but hurt self-esteem. I know what I'm doing and I don't need an onlooker's approval."
—B.P.

The Emotional Journey of Parenting An ADHD Child

Parenting an ADHD child may be an emotionally charged experience. Parents may experience a range of emotions following a diagnosis, including relief at finding a reason for their child's behaviours, regret for not recognising the indications sooner, and anxiety for the future.

As they go about their everyday lives, parents frequently experience irritation and tiredness from continually controlling their children's behaviours and coping with the repercussions of impulsivity or inattention. They may feel alone or judged by others who are unfamiliar with the challenges of ADHD, leading to feelings of loneliness or inadequacy.

However, this road also includes times of great joy and pride. It may be highly fulfilling for parents to watch their children overcome hurdles, learn new skills, or express their distinct creativity. Parents' experiences frequently lead to more empathy and perseverance.

Parents must identify and address their own emotional needs. Seeking therapy, support groups, or networking with other parents of ADHD children can provide significant emotional support as well as practical assistance.

"Having a high IQ or being intelligent does not mean ADHD is
not a disability." —Y.T.

The importance of early intervention.

*Early intervention is crucial for controlling ADHD and
increasing long-term outcomes in children. The sooner
ADHD is discovered and treated, the better-equipped
children and families will be to manage its obstacles
and maximise its potential strengths.*

Early intervention usually takes a multifaceted approach:

1. *Professional Evaluation: A thorough evaluation by healthcare specialists can help establish an accurate diagnosis and rule out other diseases that may resemble ADHD symptoms.*

2. *Behavioural Therapy: Techniques such as positive reinforcement, time management, and organisational methods can assist youngsters in developing important coping mechanisms.*

3. *Educational Support: Collaborating with schools to establish accommodations and individualised education plans can boost academic performance and self esteem.*

4. *Medication Management: In some circumstances, medication may help with symptom management, but only under close physician supervision.*

5. *Parent Training: Programs that educate parents on particular skills for dealing with ADHD behaviours can significantly enhance family dynamics and kid results.*

"Even close family members don't understand. They think that
my daughter is just spoiled. They don't spend countless hours
reading and researching and trying different things to find what
works and what doesn't." —C.A.

*Early intervention not only aids in the management of
current symptoms but also the prevention of secondary
problems caused by untreated ADHD, such as academic
failure, low self-esteem, social difficulties, and risk-
taking behaviours.*

Furthermore, early intervention can assist children with ADHD in developing a positive self-image and resilience. By addressing problems early on, children might learn to see ADHD as a different way of thinking with distinct skills and abilities.

Finally, recognising ADHD, navigating the emotional path of parenting, and embracing early intervention are the cornerstones of good ADHD parenting. This method enables parents to support their children's growth, advocate for their needs, and create an atmosphere where children with ADHD can thrive and realise their full potential.

TWO
200 TIPS FOR PARENTS

"Sportsman of the Century" and "Undisputed Boxing Champion" Muhammad Ali achieved the impossible — more than once. Don't let naysayers keep you from going after your dreams.

❥❥❥

*1. Recognise that ADHD is a neurological disorder,
not a behavioural choice.*

2. Be patient; frustration won't help.

3. Learn about ADHD and its many forms.

4. Establish structure and consistency at home.

5. Plan a daily schedule for your youngster.

6. Establish clear expectations for behaviour.

7. Use visual schedules to plan the day's activities.

*8. Break down more significant activities into smaller,
more doable steps.*

9. Avoid offering several directions at once.

10. Use concise, straightforward, and direct language.

Neurotypical doesn't mean "normal" or "better," so don't let the world tell you it does. Take advantage of

your special ability to enjoy life, even when it's not all sunshine and rainbows. Learn to love all the special talents ADHD opens up to you.

● ● ●

11. *Provide options to offer your child a sense of control.*

12. *Establish realistic goals for behaviour and success.*

13. *Recognise work, not just achievement.*

14. *Focus on your strengths rather than your faults.*

15. *Set up a reward scheme for positive behaviour.*

16. *Use positive reinforcement regularly.*

17. Instead of punishing people, employ reasonable consequences.

●

18. Create a quiet space for doing homework or relaxing.

19. Keep distractions to a minimum in your workspace.

20. Use timers to assist in managing your tasks.

*"ADHD is not a disability, it's a different ability." -
Edward M. Hallowell*

21. Divide schoolwork into shorter periods.

22. *Encourage regular pauses.*

23. *Set visible reminders for crucial activities or deadlines.*

24. *Set a consistent bedtime routine.*

25. *Limit screen time, particularly before bedtime.*

26. *Engage in physical exercises to release energy.*

27. *Encourage outdoor play wherever possible.*

28. *Provide sensory toys or fidgets to improve concentration.*

29. *Teach meditation and breathing techniques.*

30. Encourage consistent physical activity.

"Everyone shines, given the right lighting." - Susan Cain

31. *Create possibilities for creative expression.*

32. *Use apps or tools to help you stay organised.*

33. *Teach self-monitoring and self-regulation skills.*

34. *Provide written directions wherever feasible.*

35. *Be patient with repeated instructions.*

36. *Use straightforward language to describe rules.*

37. *Provide visual aids and checklists for tasks.*

38. *Celebrate tiny accomplishments every day.*

39. Set aside specific hours for homework and housework.

• 20 •

40. Give gentle reminders of the time remaining for chores.

"I can't change the direction of the wind, but I can adjust my sails to always reach my destination." - Jimmy Dean

41. Help your youngster prioritise tasks.

42. Start teaching time management skills early on.

43. Limit your intake of sugar and processed meals.

44. Maintain a balanced diet rich in brain-boosting foods.

45. Provide protein-rich snacks to help you focus.

46. Encourage hydration, particularly during school hours.

47. Be aware of food sensitivities.

48. Avoid coffee and energy drinks.

49. Teach appropriate stress-management skills.

50. Use role-playing to practise social interactions.

"ADHD isn't a bad thing, it's a different way of thinking." - David Neeleman

51. Increase emotional intelligence by labelling emotions.

*52. Help your child recognise and express his or her
emotions.*

53. Practice relaxation techniques together.

54. Use humour to diffuse stressful situations.

*55. Remain cool amid your child's emotional
outbursts.*

56. Engage in empathy and active listening.

57. Introduce deep breathing and relaxation exercises.

*58. Encourage positive behaviour with affection and
appreciation.*

*59. Practice frequent positive affirmations to boost
your self-esteem.*

60. Avoid screaming, as this can aggravate the problem.

"Quiet people have the loudest minds." - Stephen Hawking

*61. Set an excellent example by regulating your own
emotions.*

62. Avoid comparing your child to others.

63. Validate your child's struggles and emotions.

*64. Don't overwhelm your child with too many
activities.*

*65. Allow your youngster to take the initiative in their
interests.*

66. Encourage friendships with patient children.

*67. Openly discuss your feelings concerning ADHD
with your youngster.*

68. *Help them understand that their brains function differently, not worse.*

• 27 •

69. *Emphasise the value of kindness and compassion.*

70. *Offer alternatives when expressing "no."*

"ADHD is not a disorder of knowing what to do; it is a disorder of doing what you know." – Russell A. Barkley

71. Create a "cool down" area for emotional management.

72. Use visual cues for relaxation (such as coloured lighting).

73. Help them make a worry or anxiety jar.

74. Schedule regular "check-ins" to discuss feelings.

75. Celebrate individuality and diversity of ideas.

76. Teach self-advocacy skills in the classroom.

77. Encourage students to take ownership of their homework.

78. Assist with the development of personal goals and action plans.

79. Teach decision-making skills for everyday scenarios.

80. Provide advice, not control, over decisions.

*"The most important thing to remember about ADHD is that it's not a matter of willpower. It's a matter of understanding, support, and strategic planning." –
Unknown*

81. Help your youngster prepare for school the night before.

82. Create an organised and clutter-free location for their possessions.

83. Teach them how to make their beds and organise their rooms.

84. Encourage the use of planners and calendars.

85. Provide visual or written steps for morning routines.

86. Use checklists to complete autonomous activities.

*87. Assign household duties to help teach
responsibility.*

*88. Utilise natural consequences to teach
responsibility.*

*89. Encourage them to reflect on their triumphs and
disappointments.*

*90. Help your youngster keep track of their
development and goals.*

"Managing ADHD is like learning to drive a car with a powerful engine. With the right guidance and tools, children can navigate their path successfully." – Unknown

91. Show how to divide long-term projects into phases.

92. Encourage involvement in team sports to foster teamwork.

93. Promote board games that require concentration and patience.

94. Encourage volunteers to develop empathy and responsibility.

95. Encourage hobbies that require focus, such as drawing or construction.

96. Teach relaxation strategies for anxiety.

97. Practice challenging social encounters to gain confidence.

98. Teach your youngster how to resolve arguments courteously.

99. *Allow your youngster to choose their own rules and rewards.*

100. *Teach the importance of tenacity and persistence.*

*"Every child with ADHD has unique gifts. Our role is
to help them see and use those gifts in their own way."
– Unknown*

101. *Be open with teachers about ADHD issues.*

102. *Request regular updates on your child's
educational progress.*

103. *If necessary, advocate for an Individualised
Education Plan (IEP).*

104. *Help your youngster create academic goals.*

105. *Promote the use of instruments such as noise-
cancelling headphones during exams.*

106. *Provide teachers with information about what
works best for your child.*

107. Set visual clocks for classroom transitions.

108. Request to sit away from distractions in class.

109. Teach self-advocacy skills by asking questions in class.

110. Maintain constant communication with your school counsellor.

"Discipline for ADHD is not about punishment but about teaching self-regulation and building understanding." – Unknown

111. Teach note-taking techniques to boost attentiveness.

112. *Encourage teachers to include activities in extended lessons.*

113. *Request instructor accommodations, such as additional time on assessments.*

114. *Work with the school to develop realistic academic expectations.*

115. *Encourage teachers to use visual aids during lessons.*

116. *Use technology, such as tablets or laptops, to help you focus.*

117. *Volunteer in the school to better understand your child's surroundings.*

118. *Collaborate with the school to identify ADHD-friendly learning practices.*

119. Help your child establish a study schedule.

120. Discuss ADHD with your child's peers to promote understanding and inclusion.

"The journey of raising a child with ADHD is a marathon, not a sprint. It requires consistent effort, empathy, and encouragement." – Unknown

● ● ●

121. Collaborate with a behavioural therapist to create a strategy.

122. Implement impulsive coping methods.

123. Teach students how to identify causes for ADHD behaviours.

124. Use an incentive system to control impulsive behaviour.

125. Practice taking turns and waiting during games.

126. Encourage contemplation following an intense outburst.

*127. Positive behaviour should be reinforced quickly
with praise.*

• 42 •

*128. Use role-playing to cope with difficult social
circumstances.*

*129. Encourage patience through slow-paced activities,
such as reading together.*

*130. Encourage people to express their emotions
through journaling or drawing.*

"An ADHD diagnosis is not a limitation; it's a different way of engaging with the world that requires a different kind of support." – Unknown

131. Introduce awareness and meditation.

132. *Use short, focused breathing exercises to relax.*

133. *Encourage physical activity to expend surplus energy.*

134. *Attend family therapy sessions as necessary.*

135. *Facilitate peer interactions with guided playdates.*

136. *Create problem-solving solutions for typical challenges.*

137. *Set clear boundaries for appropriate behaviour.*

138. *Model acceptable behaviour.*

139. *Use humour to ease uncomfortable circumstances.*

140. Seek expert guidance as needed.

"Every child with ADHD has a different path, and with the right support, they can navigate it with confidence and success." – Unknown

141. Concentrate on improving sleep quality.

142. Establish a consistent sleep schedule.

143. Use white noise devices or peaceful music to help
you sleep.

144. Encourage physical activity throughout the day.

145. Incorporate yoga and stretching to improve
attention.

146. Exercise might help you release energy before a
task.

147. Consider alternative therapies like acupuncture
or neurofeedback.

148. Consume brain-boosting foods such as fish,

almonds, and seeds.

149. *Limit processed foods, particularly those containing artificial colours and preservatives.*

150. *Encourage a healthy diet rich in fresh vegetables and fruits.*

"Children with ADHD need patience and understanding, not just rules and discipline. They need guidance to harness their boundless energy." – Unknown

151. *Investigate mindfulness exercises to alleviate stress.*

152. *Encourage regular appointments with a paediatrician for ADHD support.*

153. *Participate in family activities to bond and develop relationships.*

154. *Maintain a peaceful home atmosphere through straightforward communication.*

155. *Limit screen time, especially for violent content.*

156. *Schedule a daily quiet time to rest.*

157. *Improve your focus by going on nature walks or engaging in outside activities.*

158. *Establish limits on social media and internet gaming.*

• 50 •

159. *Encourage creative activities like art, dancing, and music.*

160. *Discuss the benefits of self-care and relaxation.*

"ADHD is not a flaw but a different way of processing the world. Embrace the differences and work together to unlock the potential." – Unknown

161. Assist your youngster in setting realistic goals for self-improvement.

162. Celebrate progress, not perfection.

*163. Encourage your youngster to communicate
openly about their difficulties.*

164. Explain the significance of self-compassion.

165. Create a caring, nonjudgmental environment.

166. Recognise efforts, not just results.

*167. Encourage your youngster to focus on their
strengths, not simply their ADHD.*

*168. Encourage healthy body image by talking about
positive role models.*

169. *Participate in activities that boost confidence, such as sports or hobbies.*

• 53 •

170. *Limit exposure to harmful content in the media or through peer relationships.*

"Supporting a child with ADHD means focusing on their strengths and creating an environment where they can excel despite their challenges." – Unknown

171. Make social skills clear, such as sharing, taking turns, and empathy.

172. Please help your child navigate diverse social situations by role-playing them.

173. Encourage your youngster to participate in organisations or groups that offer structured activities.

174. Encourage group activities that involve collaboration, such as team sports and group projects.

175. Help your youngster identify nonverbal social indicators such as body language and facial expressions.

176. *Teach your child how to initiate discussions by asking questions.*

• 55 •

177. *Encourage friendships by scheduling playdates or group outings.*

178. *Encourage involvement in organised extracurricular activities with clear rules and expectations.*

179. *Emphasise the necessity of apologising when appropriate and admitting responsibility.*

180. *Discussing concerns with your child can help him or her develop conflict-resolution skills.*

*"When managing ADHD, it's important to remember
that progress is often gradual. Celebrate small
victories and keep moving forward." – Unknown*

*181. Teach the concept of "personal space" and how to
respect others' limits.*

182. Help them understand when it is good to listen and when to speak.

183. Foster empathy by exploring how others might feel in specific situations.

184. Help your youngster understand that making errors is a natural learning process.

185. Demonstrate proper social behaviours during family events and trips.

186. Encourage the usage of polite phrases like "please" and "thank you."

187. Teach your youngster to make eye contact throughout chats, which promotes social connection.

188. Recognise good social interactions and specific beneficial behaviours.

189. *Teach your child the difference between harmless teasing and cruel statements.*

190. *Foster friendships with patients and understanding supportive peers.*

"When managing ADHD, it's important to remember that progress is often gradual. Celebrate small victories and keep moving forward." – Unknown

191. Limit your social media use, which can occasionally lead to unfavourable interactions.

192. Help your child deal with disappointment when social events are unplanned.

193. Encourage collaborative games and projects that promote teamwork and communication.

194. Teach your youngster the importance of sharing responsibility in group settings.

195. Practice practical listening skills and model them for others.

196. Encourage positive social relationships through

praise and prizes.

197. Please help your child set goals for strengthening their social skills, such as establishing one new friend.

198. Create a social storybook containing incidents and acceptable reactions.

199. Participate in social skills training programs or therapy as needed.

200. Celebrate social victories, no matter how little, and provide suggestions for growth.

"Empathy is key in managing ADHD. Understand their challenges and work with them to find solutions that work for their unique needs." – Unknown

❧❧❧

❧❧❧

By following these thorough guidelines, parents can assist their ADHD children in developing greater self-regulation, social skills, and academic techniques. The ultimate goal is to help ADHD youngsters succeed in their circumstances while preserving their talents and abilities. Balancing structure and compassion, fostering social ties and encouraging positive behaviour can significantly advance a child's emotional and cognitive development. Every child is unique, and effective ADHD parenting requires patience, consistency, and understanding.

About The Author

Dheeraj Mehrotra, MS, MPhil, PhD (Education Management)., a white and a yellow belt in SIX SIGMA, a Certified NLP Business Diploma holder, is an Educational Innovator, Author, with expertise in Six Sigma In Education, Academic Audits, Neuro-Linguistic Programming (NLP), Total Quality Management In Education, an Experiential Educator, a CBSE Resource towards School Assessment (SQAA), CCE, JIT, Five S, and KAIZEN. He has authored over 100 books on computer science, AI, digital body language, NLP, quality circles, school management, classroom effectiveness, and safety and security. A former Principal at De Indian Public School, New Delhi, (INDIA), NPS International School, Guwahati, and Education Officer at GEMS, Gurgaon, with ample teaching experience of over Three Decades, he is a certified Trainer for Quality Circles/ TQM in Education and QCI Standards for School Accreditation/ School Audits and Management. He has also been honoured with the President of India's National Teacher Award in 2006 and the Best Science Teacher State Award (By the Ministry of Science and Technology, State of UP), Innovation in Education for his inception of Six Sigma In Education by Education Watch, New Delhi and Education World- Best Teacher Award, BOLT Learner Teacher Award by Air India, 'Innovation in Education Award 2016' by Higher Education Forum (HEF), Gujarat Chapter, among others. He has developed over 150 FREE EDUCATIONAL MOBILE Apps for the Google Play Store exclusively for Teachers, Students, and Parents. This work has been recognised by the LIMCA BOOK OF RECORDS and INDIA BOOK OF RECORDS as the only Indian to draw that feast. As a founder president of the IoT Society of India, he also promotes Technology Globally. Dr Mehrotra is presently engaged as a PRINCIPAL at KUNWARS GLOBAL SCHOOL, Lucknow, India. He has conducted over 2000 workshops globally on "Excellence In Education" integrated with Total Quality Management and Six Sigma, Technology Integration in Education (TIE), Developing towards being ROCKSTAR TEACHERS, including Cyberspace, Cyber Security, Classroom Management, School Leadership & Management, and Innovative teaching within classrooms via Mind Maps, NLP and Experiential Learning in Academics. He is an active TEDx speaker and can be viewed on the YouTube TEDx channel. As a premium UDEMY Instructor, he has developed over 500 courses and caters to over 8 Lakh students from 180 countries. He can be visited at www.authordheerajmehrotra.com

www.authordheerajmehrotra.com

Books By The Same Author

Towards Quality Literacy For
Allwww.authordheerajmehrotra.com